WHERE HAVE
ALL THE
SARDINES
GONE?

by
Randall A. Reinstedt

cover illustration by
Antone Hrusa

If bookstores in your area do not carry "WHERE HAVE ALL THE SARDINES GONE?", copies may be obtained by writing to . . .

GHOST TOWN PUBLICATIONS

P.O. Drawer 5998
Carmel, CA 93921

Other books by Randall A. Reinstedt, offered by Ghost Town Publications, are:

Second Printing

Library of Congress Number: 79-101716
ISBN 0-933818-05-X

COLOR-AD PRINTERS • MONTEREY

2

This book is dedicated to the sardine fishermen and to the pioneer residents who made Monterey "the sardine capital of the world".

Contents

Introduction

"**W**here Have All the Sardines Gone?" has been published as a pictorial introduction to the colorful history of the Monterey waterfront and its famed sardine fishing industry. Unfortunately, in a volume of this size and format, it is impossible to tell the complete story and give due credit to the countless individuals who had a part in bringing the coveted title of "the sardine capital of the world" to old Monterey.

With this in mind, the author has kept the text brief and has only attempted to summarize the colorful story of Monterey's fishing industry. Included in the work are sketches of the early years when men like Frank E. Booth, Knute Hovden and Pietro "Pete" Ferrante combined their talents to develop the infant sardine industry. With this as a beginning, the text continues with brief accounts of the development of Cannery Row, the building of Monterey's picturesque wharves, the coming of the purse seiner, 200,000-ton seasons, the hardships and heartaches of the men of the sea, the disappearance of the silvery sardine and, of course, John Steinbeck and his part in making Cannery Row what it is today.

In keeping the text brief and to the point, the author's desire has been to let the pictures tell the story. Firmly believing in the old adage that "a picture is worth a thousand words", the author has spent considerable time in assembling a vast Monterey waterfront and sardine industry oriented picture collection. In carefully selecting the most representative of the pictures, he has contented himself with letting the pictures do the talking. Pains have been taken to insure the captions are accurate, but even after checking and rechecking (with those in the know), discrepancies most assuredly will be noted, and mistakes will be spotted. With this in mind, the author wishes to apologize in advance for any misspelled or deleted names, and for any misquoted dates, figures, and/or facts. With much of the information coming from aged, and perhaps exaggerated, newspaper accounts, and from the somewhat faded memories of old-timers, it would be unrealistic to think that each and every utterance or "documented statement" was without question. Nevertheless, it is hoped by the author that "Where Have All the Sardines Gone?" will be accepted for what it was meant to be — a brief pictorial history —

6

and will be enjoyed by all who read it. . . especially by the veteran sardine fishermen who cherish their memories, and call Monterey home.

Acknowledgements

*A*s with past books, it is a difficult task to acknowledge each and every individual who has donated time, told a tale, tracked down aged newspapers, opened family diaries, loaned prized photographs and, sometimes most important of all, has had an encouraging word to say along the way.

Also, as with past books, without these countless people and their willingness to share all they had and all they knew, "Where Have All the Sardines Gone?" could not have been written. It is to these people that the real credit for this work should be given. In continuing with the subject of credit, the author wishes to stress that all photographs have been credited to the collection, or source, from which they were obtained. When known, the photographer's name is also included. It is the all-important photographers, known and unknown — living or dead, that have made the book what it is. Without their work and interest long ago, a pictorial history such as this would not have been possible.

In attempting to acknowledge the many who have contributed — above and beyond the call of duty — the author wishes to thank Vincent J. Bruno, Gaspar V. Cardinale, Robert Blaisdell, Tom R. Russo, Anita M. (Maiorana) Ferrante, Vincent Colletto, Pat Hathaway, John N. Crivello, Ruth Fisher, Dorothy Ronald, Frank J. Nuovo, Jessie Sandholdt, Mary Sherman, Jack Stracuzzi, Kevin Ford, Salvatore A. Ferrante, Werner Papenhoefer, John "Bricky" Crivello, Tony R. Souza, James A. Gruber, Admiral Earl E. Stone (of Monterey's Allen Knight Maritime Museum), and Marilyn Rodrock.

Along the way countless other people have expressed interest, added their comments (and corrections), and in their own special way have helped to make the book as meaningful as it is. It is to these people, and especially to those mentioned above, that the author is truly indebted and to whom he extends his heartfelt thanks.

Lastly, to Debbie, Erick and Joshua (his understanding English bulldog), the author once again wishes to say "Thank you!".

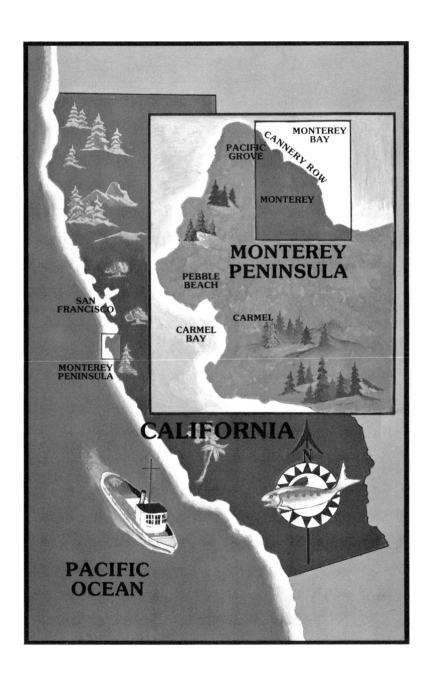

MONTEREY
BAY

PACIFIC
GROVE

CANNERY ROW

MONTEREY

MONTEREY
PENINSULA

PEBBLE
BEACH

SAN
FRANCISCO

MONTEREY
PENINSULA

CARMEL
BAY

CARMEL

CALIFORNIA

N

PACIFIC
OCEAN

8

CANNERY ROW

MONTEREY BAY

BREAKWATER

FISHERMAN'S WHARF

WHARF NO. 2

The maps on these two pages were created by Carmel artist Antone Hrusa and are meant to help familiarize the reader with the location of California's famed Monterey Peninsula..., and of its historic wharf and Cannery Row areas.

CANNERY ROW 1946

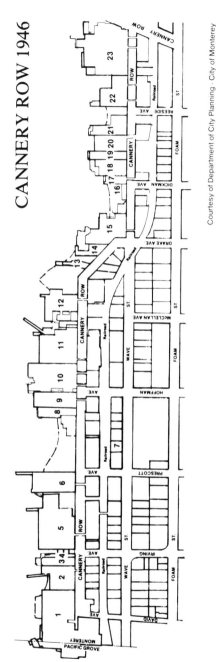

Courtesy of Department of City Planning - City of Monterey

LEGEND

1. Howden Food Products Corp.
2. Atlantic Coast Fisheries Co.
3. Monterey Fish Products Inc.
4. Del Vista Packing Co.
5. Del Mar Canning Co.
6. Monterey Canning Co.
7. Edgewater Packing Co.
8. Sea Beach Packing Co.

9. Custom House Packing Corp.
10. Carmel Canning Co.
11. California Packing Corp.
12. San Xavier Fish Packing Co.
13. Western Sardine Co., Inc.
14. Ferrante Co.
15. Oxnard Canners, Inc.
16. Wester Fish Products Corp.

17. Aenas Sardine Packing Co.
18. Central Packing Co.
19. Ronada Fisheries & Manola Packing Co.
20. Enterprise Packers
21. California Frozen Fish Co.
22. Peninsula Packing Co.
23. San Carlos Canning Co.

WHERE HAVE ALL THE SARDINES GONE?

Monterey By The Bay

For some the history of Monterey had its start in the long-ago year of 1542, as that was the year historians credit the Portuguese navigator Juan Rodriquez Cabrillo with having been the first European to spot central California's rounded bay. Others feel Francis Drake, the English privateer (who has been credited by a select few with having made a brief call on the lonely California Peninsula in 1579), was the first "outsider" to set foot on Monterey soil. They therefore claim Monterey's history should begin with Drake and this four-century-old port-of-call. Still others feel it was the naming of Monterey Bay in 1602 by the Spanish explorer Sebastian Vizcaino that launched the colorful and romantic history of Monterey and its picturesque bay. Finally, for history buffs of California's famed mission period, the year 1770 is considered the Peninsula's historic starting point. It was in this year that the diminutive Franciscan padre, Father Junipero Serra, and his military commander, Gaspar de Portola, officially founded the community of Monterey — a community that was destined to become the capital city of the Alta California territory.

From this point on in history one can document countless events that have come and gone, and in their own special way have made Monterey the unique and history-rich village by the bay that it is. One could dwell on the year 1818 when the dreaded Pacific pirate Hippolyte Bouchard attacked and sacked the capital city. Perhaps to others the year 1846 was of paramount importance as it was in this year that Monterey was captured by American forces, bringing it and an additional 600,000 square miles under the rule of the red, white and blue. In 1850, it was Monterey that hosted the blustery constitutional convention, paving the way for California to become the United States' thirty-first state.

In 1880 the magic of Monterey was once again the talk of the land, as travelers from throughout the world lavishly praised the

11

opulent Hotel Del Monte that had opened its doors on the southerly shore of the rounded bay. Described as "the most elegant seaside establishment in the world", and hosting personalities from various corners of the globe, the fame of the Hotel Del Monte continued to spread. . . with it and the beautiful Monterey Peninsula soon becoming "the places to see and be seen" by the wealthy of the world.

As one continues to document the history of the Monterey Peninsula, and lists events that have played important parts in making it what it is today, he cannot overlook the year 1900 as it was this turn-of-the-century year that marked the moving to Monterey of Frank E. Booth. Booth, who had been a frequent visitor to the bayside community long before his move, had consistently been impressed by the number of sardines that abounded in the blue waters of the bay. At the time of his sojourns to the Monterey area, Booth and his father were involved in the canning of salmon in their Pittsburg (California) plant. It was this background in the canning and packing of fish that prompted Booth to ponder the possibility of canning the abundant Monterey Bay sardine. Upon his move to the bayside community, Booth founded the F.E. Booth Company in a plant near the aged and historic Monterey Custom House. It was the founding of this company and the building of the plant that, in a very literal sense, was the beginning of Monterey's famed sardine industry.

Not long after Booth launched the California sardine as a commercially canned product, a second man who, along with Booth, was destined to become an important figure in Monterey's multi-million-dollar sardine industry, arrived on the local scene. Knute Hovden, a recent immigrant from Norway, a graduate of the Norwegian National Fisheries College, and a skillfully trained professional in the fish packing field, teamed up with Booth, and between these two turn-of-the-century pioneers the highly competitive and extremely profitable Monterey Bay sardine canning industry continued to develop and expand.

With Booth and Hovden perfecting the canning phase of Monterey's infant sardine industry, the time soon came when the biggest problem they faced was getting a steady supply of fish. With the ability to handle five tons of sardines per day, and with the daily catch being highly erratic due to the fishing methods that were currently being used (combined with the questionable skill of many of the local fishermen), Booth and Hovden decided their next project must be to find a way to increase and insure the size of the daily catch.

A Man Called Pete

At this point in history, a man who was eventually to become one of Monterey's best known and most respected citizens arrived on the scene. Pietro Ferrante, born on the island of Sicily (Italy) in 1867 and affectionately called "Pete" by all who knew him, was this man. By the time Ferrante arrived in Monterey in 1904 he had many years of fishing experience behind him, and had gained a reputation as a man of vision as well as a man of considerable fishing talent. With Booth, Hovden and Ferrante all in the area at the same time, and all realizing the untapped potential of the Monterey Bay sardine, it was only natural that they would soon get together.

After analyzing the problem and observing the methods of fishing that were being used, Ferrante voiced the opinion that a whole new approach to the catching of sardines was needed if they were to truly reap the bounty of the bay. With this in mind, and thinking back to the lampara boat and net method of fishing he had been familiar with as a boy in the distant Mediterranean, it did not take Ferrante long to redesign the lampara net and adapt it for use in the deep water bay of Monterey. (For those unfamiliar with the lampara net, briefly, it is a net that will encircle an entire school of fish, enabling the fish to be brought to the lampara boat where they can be taken from the water. The word lampara was derived from the Italian word lampo — meaning lightning — because the net was designed for a fast cast and haul.)

After demonstrating the practicality of the lampara net to several local skeptics (including many of Monterey's fishermen), and after being given the go-ahead by Booth, Ferrante sent word to his Italian fishermen friends in Sicily, Pittsburg and along California's Sacramento River, urging them to come to Monterey and join him in the hunt for sardines. Heeding the call, many of Ferrante's friends and relatives ventured to the rounded bay. . . and, as it has been stated so often, it was the arrival of the skilled Italian fishermen that started Monterey on its way to becoming a major fishing port.

(In fairness to all, it should be stated that even though Pietro Ferrante is credited in most sources as being the "father" of Monterey's famed fishing fraternity, there were many other pioneer fishermen who played an important part in the early development of Monterey's fishing industry.)

13

Fish, Fame And Fortune

ith the aid of the lampara net, and with the knowledge and skill of the newly arrived fishermen, the sleepy bayside community began to experience a somewhat gradual, but certainly significant change. By 1913 the canning industry, with its carefully developed techniques and modernized mode of operation, was described as having "come of age", and was no longer looked upon as being in the crude and experimental stage. In keeping up with the canners, the fishing boat crews (which usually consisted of six highly trained workers), were catching as much as twenty-five tons of sardines in a single night. (Those unfamiliar with the techniques used by the sardine fishermen may be surprised to learn that the ideal fishing conditions were on dark moonless nights. It was under these conditions that the fishermen could best spot the phosphorescent glow of a school of sardines and, in turn, know where to place their nets.)

With the supply of fish no longer a problem, Hovden decided to branch out on his own, and in 1914 he opened a cannery on what was then a picturesque and uncluttered stretch of Monterey beach. With others to follow, it was not long before this unspoiled shoreline was to become lined with the clutter, the noise, and the smell of several smoke-belching canneries. By 1918 Monterey boasted a total of nine canning plants and packed a total of 1,400,000 cases of sardines. . . , as compared to a mere 75,000 cases a short three years before! At this point in history, with canneries continuing to spring up at an astonishing rate, and with fish being caught by the hundreds of tons, people did not concern themselves with saving scenic shorelines. It was not long before the once picturesque stretch of Monterey beach (now known as Cannery Row), was lost forever to industry and progress. . . and the over-abundant sardine.

The early 1920s were the peak years of the lampara boat and net method of fishing, as 1925 brought the introduction of the half-ring net. Over the years the size of the lampara boats had kept pace with the expanding industry and had increased in size along with their specially designed lighters (tow barges in which to haul their catch). Rather than small and awkward, as many of the original boats had been, the newer boats reached lengths of forty feet and boasted trim lines as well as dependable motors.

With the introduction of the half-ring net, the half-ring boat also

14

appeared. This boat differed only slightly from the lampara boat as, among other things, it boasted a winch, a mast, and a boom. With the use of the rings, from which the half-ring net and boat got their names, many more fish could be caught per haul as the net rings pursed (or pocketed) the net, thus trapping the fish and making it difficult for them to escape.

With time marching on, the lampara boats, as well as the more efficient half-ring boats, became outmoded with the introduction of a vessel bearing a name that at one time was almost synonymous with the name Monterey. This vessel was the purse seiner. The popular purse seiner took its name from the type of net it carried which, when full of trapped fish, formed a purse. With the word seine describing the type of net commonly used by the sardine fishermen, it is not difficult to understand how the vessel became known as a purse seiner. Varying in size, the largest of the purse seiners approached the 100-foot mark and carried nets that were capable of encircling a football field in width, and drop to a depth equaling the height of a ten-story building when in the water. This new breed of boat was also capable of fishing hundred of miles at sea and carrying between 140 and 150 tons of fish in its hold. With the introduction of the purse seiner, and the elimination of the lighter, sardine fishing in and around the Monterey Bay area took on an added dimension.

Through the thirties and on into the early forties the Monterey fishing fleet and its supporting cast of canneries continued to grow and prosper. In 1930 the catch was 159,000 tons; by 1935 it had jumped to 230,000 tons, and during the early forties there were years when the catch approached the almost unbelievable figure of a quarter of a million tons!

With the supply of fish being constant and abundant, cannery operators had long since learned that not only was there money to be made in the canning of fish, but in the processing of fish by-products as well. With fish meal becoming widely used for poultry and livestock feed, as well as being in demand as fertilizer, the oil from the fish (which at one time was considered waste) was sought after for use in the manufacture of soap, paint mixer, vitamins, glycerine (for ammunition), shortening, salad oil and the tanning of leather. By 1945, considered by many to have been the zenith year of the local fishing industry, Monterey boasted 19 canneries and 20 reduction plants (for the development of fish by-products). The fishing fleet numbered well over 100, with 84 of the vessels being of the purse seiner variety. It was during this period that Monterey was known as the sardine capital of the world, and in total tonnage it ranked third among the world's major fishing ports (second only to Stavanger, Norway and Hull, England).

A Tale Of Inches

In an attempt to dramatize the enormous number of sardines that were delivered to Cannery Row during a good year, a tale of inches (with the Monterey Peninsula Herald providing the statistics) proves quite effective. 1939, the year from which the statistics are quoted, boasted a season catch of 215,000 tons. In figuring 2,000 pounds to the ton, one soon discovers that the 215,000 ton catch equals 430,000,000 pounds of sardines. With the 1939 catch averaging approximately three fish to the pound, the 430,000,000 pounds of fish represents a staggering 1,290,000,000 individual sardines! While this figure seems more at home in our current age of calculators and computers than it did in the long-ago year of 1939, the following figures become even more remarkable.

By calculating the average length of the sardine caught during the 1939 season as being in the 10-inch category (although many were considerably larger), one only need multiply the number of individual sardines by 10 (representing the average length — in inches — per fish) to arrive at a grand total of 12,900,000,000 inches! If this astronomical figure were to be divided by twelve (the number of inches in a foot), we would discover that the 215,000-ton 1939 catch (if, of course, the sardines were placed end to end), would equal a distance of 1,075,000,000 feet. By again dividing, this time by 5,280 (the number of feet in a mile), we would learn that our row of sardines would stretch a distance of 203,600 miles. . . or, perhaps more dramatically stated, a distance nearly equal to that of from the earth to the moon!

Carrying this project one step further, we find that if our row of ten-inch sardines (which would certainly be a bit smelly by now) were laid end to end in a line that stretched around the world (at the equator), they would circle the earth eight times. . . with over 3,600 miles of fish left over!

In bringing this exercise in frustration to a close, it should be mentioned that, fortunately, the majority of sardine aficionados of 1939 were not interested in stretching sardines from here to eternity, and preferred to lay these tempting morsels from the sea in clusters, on a plate, enabling them to enjoy the true taste and talent of the Monterey Bay sardine.

All Was Not Glory

As Monterey's sardine industry continued to grow and prosper, there were also many minuses that had to be counted along with the pluses. In the long-ago year of 1903, as the infant sardine industry was getting its start, the F.E. Booth canning plant mysteriously burned down. The blame for this foul deed fell on local fishermen who were described as not liking Booth, his sardines, or the smell of his cannery. Undaunted by the fire, Booth resumed operations in a nearby smokehouse. Upon opening a saloon adjacent to the smokehouse, Booth served fish along with schooners of beer. From that point on in the annals of local history, Booth's sardines were known as "soused mackerel". A fire also destroyed the cannery of Knute Hovden in 1921. As with the Booth fire, arson was suspected. It was not long after the fire that an ex-convict was captured and convicted, with Hovden claiming a rival canner had hired the "ex-con" to put the torch to his plant. As with Booth, Hovden was not a man to give up easily, and it wasn't long before a bigger and better cannery rose from the ashes.

As the years rolled on, other fires came and other canneries were destroyed. (In 1951 the Westgate-Sun Harbor cannery and warehouse went up in flames, destroying $1,500,000 worth of canned fish in the process. When the blaze was over and the loss was tallied, it was listed as the third largest food fire in United States history.)

If it wasn't fires destroying canneries, it was unpredictable storms unleashing their fury on the fleet (with the storms of 1915, 1919, 1943 and 1953 being among the best remembered). Even during the "good times" when no fires or storms caused heartache or grief, there were the dreaded recessions that caused canneries to go bankrupt or to change hands. To add to the woe of the canners and fishermen, there were also the residents and merchants of the Monterey area (who were not dependent upon the sardine for survival) who annually complained to city hall of the odors and pollution created by the canneries and the reduction plants. Problems within the industry itself also created considerable difficulties as each year boat owners, fishermen, cannery owners, and cannery workers somehow had to be brought together in an agreement on wages. This difficult-to-answer question revolved around the "projected" availability of the sardine. Being a yearly ritual along the waterfront, the animated discussions and countless meetings usually created considerable fist waving and the burning of much midnight oil. Skullduggery was also an unfortunate part of the local scene as, among other underhanded schemes, deals were sometimes made between boat owners and canners whereby overlimit catches were overlooked.

One could go on with the problems and frustrations of Monterey's sardine industry, but, as one old-timer aptly put it, "why pop a bubble that has already burst?"

Where Have All The Sardines Gone?

With 1945 being remembered as the high point of Monterey's sardine industry, it should also be stated that 1946 marked the beginning of the low point for the very same industry. Although fish continued to be caught and canneries continued to work, the handwriting was on the wall and it was clearly written for all to see. Comparison figures show the 1946 catch to have been nearly 100,000 tons under the 1945 mark, with the 1947 catch being over 100,000 tons less than that. This put the catch in the neighborhood of 27,000 tons, with the 1948 catch plummeting to a disastrous 14,000 tons (with much of that being trucked to the Monterey canneries from more abundant fishing grounds to the south).

As the cash flow from the prosperous sardine industry dropped to a mere trickle, thousands of people and countless businesses throughout the Peninsula felt the pinch.

With optimism at its low point as the 1949 season approached, the industry — for reasons unknown — received a most welcome shot in the arm as the catch jumped to 41,000 tons. As the 1950 season rolled around, thousands of Peninsulans held their breaths and crossed their fingers. . . hoping and praying that the unpredictable sardine would once again return to central California waters. As if bowing to their wishes and answering their prayers, the sardine arrived on schedule — enabling the fleet to record a catch of 132,000 tons! Even though the 1950 catch was over 100,000 tons less than the catch of 1945, the industry's dollar turnover was the greatest in its history. As the 1950 season came to a close. . . for all intents and purposes, so did Monterey's sardine industry. The 1951 catch was

18

embarrassingly small, and by 1952 canneries were folding at such a rapid rate that only a brief mention of their closing made the local papers.

As the canneries closed (with many selling their equipment at a fraction of its original cost to canneries in such distant places as Venezuela and South Africa), many of the purse seiners found their way to various southland ports where sardines were still frolicking in the sea.

With the harbor relatively empty of purse seiners and much of Cannery Row on the auction block, Monterey's sardine industry became little more than a memory. Millions had been made during the rowdy and robust days of the sardine, and millions had been lost as the industry went from boom to bust in less than a fifty-year span. As one looks back at the color and pageantry of Monterey's sardine industry, the haunting question of "where have all the sardines gone?" remains a mystery to many. . . , while others shake their heads and talk about polluted waters, warmer climates, changes in currents, recurring cycles and, of course, the distinct possibility that the once-abundant sardine was just plain fished out.

Along Came John

Even though the bubble that was Monterey's mighty sardine industry began to deflate after the peak year of 1945, a second chapter in the colorful life along the Monterey waterfront began to take shape in that very same year. Among other events that marked 1945 as a year to remember on the Monterey Peninsula, was the publication of a book called "Cannery Row" by the Salinas-born author John Steinbeck. (The community of Salinas is approximately twenty miles east of Monterey.) Internationally known in the field of literature, and locally known as a man who enjoyed "the good life", Steinbeck's story of the color and characters along what was then Ocean View Avenue became so popular, and focused so much attention on the mile-long stretch of corrugated tin, tilted smoke stacks and eye-catching walkways high above the street, that the City of Monterey (in 1953) officially changed the name of the cannery-lined street to Cannery Row.

With Steinbeck's book immortalizing the Row as "a poem, a stink, a grating noise, a quality of light, a tone, a habit, a nostalgia" and "a dream", it was inevitable that the curious would come to take a look for themselves. Such landmark sites as Doc Rickett's Lab, Wing Chong's Market, the overgrown lot where Mack and the boys dreamed the days away and of course, the popular Lone Star where Flora and the girls practiced the "oldest profession", all became known and revered sites to lovers of Steinbeckien lore. With the tourists coming in ever increasing numbers, and the sardines staying away in equally increasing numbers (the come-back years of 1949-50 being the exceptions), the business-oriented people of Monterey began looking toward the silver of the coins disgorged by the visitors, rather than the silver of the sardine that for so many years meant prosperity and security to the people of the Peninsula.

There Is More To The Waterfront Than Old Cannery Row

More unique to many than its Row or its collection of historic buildings is Monterey's popular Fisherman's Wharf. Described as the most picturesque of all Pacific Coast piers, the story of Fisherman's Wharf (as well as Monterey's other docks and piers), is an interesting chapter in Monterey history. To get the full benefit of the colorful growth of the Monterey waterfront, one must look back to the year 1845. It was in this long-ago year that Thomas O. Larkin (the U.S. Counsul to California) decided it was time California's capital city (a title Monterey then claimed) had a wharf. Thinking it inappropriate that visitors arriving by sea should be forced to jump from launches and wade through breakers in their efforts to reach the Monterey shore, and fully aware that docking facilities would help immeasurably with the loading and unloading of merchandise from his nearby store, the industrious Larkin decided to finance construction of a capital city pier. The completion of said pier enabled Monterey to boast California's first wharf. Located in the vicinity of the present-day Fisherman's Wharf, Larkin's 1845 pier stretched a realtively short distance into the sea, and cost its builder an estimated $8,000 (aged accounts state Larkin paid $1,500 for 1,500 cartloads of rock and $4.00 for each wooden piling that was used).

Records are somewhat vague as to what became of California's first dock, as the next mention of wharves along the Monterey waterfront states that in 1868 the Pacific Coast Steamship Company began construction of a second wharf "where the first once stood".

Completed in 1870, the Steamship Company pier was 400 feet in length and boasted a freight warehouse and Steamship Company office at its seaward end. Upon its completion the Pacific Coast Steamship Company inaugurated a freight and passenger service to the Monterey Peninsula, with ships calling at their new south bay facility on a four-times-per-week basis.

In 1874 Monterey was blessed with a second pier and a railroad as well. The coming of the railroad to Monterey was another important first for the village by the bay, as the newly-formed Monterey and Salinas Valley Railroad Company was the first narrow gauge railroad to be built in California.

Upon completion of the railroad line, the company built a 1,300-foot pier in front of its depot (where the Monterey Marina is now located). Although the railroad was relatively short lived (eventually bowing to the mighty Southern Pacific), its narrow pier remained intact (with periodic repairs and rebuilding) until 1940 when it was removed.

As the years rolled on, other piers such as the Bathhouse pier of the famed Hotel Del Monte, the Booth Cannery pier, and the Coalinga Oil and Transportation Company Wharf (better known as the Associated Oil Company pier), were built in and about the Monterey waterfront. Even though each of the piers served a purpose and hummed with activity, the original Pacific Coast Steamship Company wharf remained the center of harbor life for the people of Monterey.

A Change Of Names And A Change Of Scenes

In 1913, with the expanding of the sardine industry and the desire to keep the Steamship Company pier in better repair, the City of Monterey "assumed ownership" of the aging wharf. It was during this period that the Steamship Company pier became known as Fisherman's Wharf. After leasing space to defray upkeep costs and help finance much needed additions, the city added a wing (in 1917) for freighter service. By 1920 the wharf boasted several warehouses, approximately 20 wholesale and retail fish outlets, a restaurant, a marine service station and an abalone shell grinding business.

In March of 1923, with the Monterey wharf stacked high with 20,000 cases of sardines (the largest load of sardines ever to have been shipped from the local port), disaster struck in the form of bad weather. As the steamship SAN ANTONIO awaited the loading of her cargo of fish, the swells and waves from the open bay caused her to "lean" too heavily on the wharf, resulting in the collapse of a 132-foot section of the pier! As the pier gave in to the crunch of the SAN ANTONIO, 9,750 cases of sardines slid into the bay. With nearly half of the $200,000 sardine payload in the choppy waters of the bay, local fishermen were summoned to salvage what they could. Working as if their lives depended on each and every case they could recover, the hard working fishermen succeeded in bringing 4,000 cases of "re-caught" sardines back to the pier. An additional 5,000 cases were salvaged by divers, resulting in the total loss of only 750 cases.

In the wharf construction that followed, the 400-foot length of the original Steamship Company pier was extended an additional 750 feet. A marine service station and a finger pier to the east were added at this time.

1925 brought a new look to the Monterey waterfront in the form of a second, and much longer, municipal wharf (built to the east of Fisherman's Wharf and the Monterey and Salinas Valley Railroad Company pier). Extending 1,750 feet into the bay, Monterey's "Wharf No. 2" was an important addition to the waterfront as it aptly met the needs of the expanding commercial fishing industry. Completed on December 31, 1926 (at a cost of $246,000), Wharf No. 2 served many purposes, including that of a cargo pier, and helped immeasurably in relieving the congestion in and around Fisherman's Wharf.

New Year's Day of 1932 marked the beginning of the long-overdue Monterey breakwater. Upon the 1934 completion of the 1,700-foot breakwater, Monterey's harbor became a much more sheltered refuge for its ever expanding fishing fleet. Unfortunately, as several illustrations contained herein (pages 123-125) graphically illustrate, the breakwater didn't completely solve the problems of fierce ocean winds and unpredictable Pacific storms.

Remember The People

O ver a quarter of a century has passed since the corrugated canneries along the Row and the sleek purse seiners that once lay at anchor in the bay brought prosperity to the people of the Peninsula. Cannery Row and the more centralized downtown Monterey waterfront have been transformed into a multitude of visitor-oriented businesses and convention facilities. Portions of the old Row are still to be seen, and certainly picturesque Fisherman's Wharf is still reminiscent of an era that has long since passed, but Monterey today. . . , as was the case prior to the sardine (when the Hotel Del Monte was the talk of the land), once again looks to its visitors to stimulate its economy. Perhaps this is as it should be, as the Monterey Peninsula has been richly blessed and has much to offer its visitors as well as its residents.

Monterey, the once sleepy village by the bay, has come of age in a new and exciting way. . . but as one looks around he can only nod and say, "History has made it what it is today". With this thought in mind the author hopes that the people who read this book, and relive a bit of Monterey's past, will appreciate the individuals, as well as the events, that have played such an important part in making Monterey the colorful community that it now is.

A Pictorial History . . .

Before beginning the picture section of this book the reader should be aware that the pictures are placed in a "staggered" date order. The date overlaps that appear are due primarily to the quantity of photographs and the subject matter they cover.

It is hoped that the reader will view the illustrations in sequence. If he does, he will see a remarkable story unfold . . . the story of a lifetime to many Montereyans.

Taken in the late 1800s, the above illustration shows the Pacific Coast Steamship Company pier, complete with its all-important freight and ticket office. It was this pier that eventually became known as Monterey's Fisherman's Wharf. The ships are unidentified, although personnel from the San Francisco Maritime Museum indicate the vessel at anchor (center) could be a U.S. sea exploration ship. P. Hathaway Collection.

The above picture of Monterey's Pacific Coast Steamship Company pier was taken at a later date than the previous photo (note power pole). The illustration is a favorite of old-timers as it clearly shows the 400-foot pier, as well as a trio of elegantly dressed ladies in their Victorian finery. Camera Masters Collection.

27

From Presidio hill one gets a different perspective of the Pacific Coast Steamship Company pier. The aged cannon in the foreground serves as a graphic reminder that "El Castillo", Spain and Mexico's "fort on the hill", once occupied this spot and protected California's capital city from intruders. The vessel at the end of the wharf is thought to be the Pacific Coast Steamship Company's coastal freighter GIPSY (wrecked on Monterey's Macabee Beach — Cannery Row — on September 27, 1905). The pier to the right of the Steamship Company wharf is the Monterey and Salinas Valley Railroad Company pier (Depot Wharf). In the distance (left) is the Bathhouse pier of the famed Hotel Del Monte (a portion of the hotel can be seen nestled in the trees above the Bathhouse pier buildings). C. Johnson photo — P. Hathaway Collection.

28

The Pacific Coast Steamship Company wharf as it appeared in September of 1900. Assorted buildings, including packing sheds, warehouses, and at least one fish market, can be seen in this turn-of-the-century photograph. P. Hathaway Collection.

With the Monterey wharf continuing to change, the above photo shows two recently completed warehouses, with the Steamship Company building in the background. The warehouse to the right is described by old-timers as having been operated by the F.E. Booth (Canning) Company. Monterey Public Library Collection.

In looking at the Booth Company warehouse (as described in the above picture) from the seaward side, one also sees boats of the salmon variety as long-ago fishermen prepare to go to sea. J. Oliver photo — Monterey Public Library Collection.

Monterey's early salmon fishing fleet presents a peaceful picture as the small boats dot the waters of Monterey Bay. P. Hathaway Collection.

An assorted group of pioneer fishermen happily pose for the photographer and humorously display their catch of squid. The picture was taken near the seaward end of Fisherman's Wharf and is said to date back to the early 1920s. Monterey Public Library Collection.

31

With power to the pier, and development continuing to take place, things were seldom quiet around Monterey's Wharf No. 1. The steamship company vessel in the background is unidentified; however, the sign on the warehouse (center) reads:

MATTEI NAPOLI
WHOLESALE — RETAIL
ALL KINDS OF FISH
SHIPMENTS TO ALL PARTS OF THE STATE

L. Josselyn photo — P. Hathaway Collection.

Whether they be called herring, pilchards, or sardines, the above photo offers proof that fish were abundant in the waters of Monterey Bay near the turn of the century. Taken in 1902, the photo shows the historic Custom House (to the left) and presents a "new look" to the entrance of Wharf No. 1, as the recently constructed Monterey Boating Club building dominates the scene. M. Oliver photo — Monterey Public Library Collection.

Closer to the wharf, and taken from approximately the same angle and at approximately the same period of time as the top photo, the above scene proves that other than fish, Monterey of the early 1900s also boasted an elegant array of grandly dressed people. Unfortunately, the festive occasion is unrecorded. Monterey Savings & Loan Association Collection.

A closer look at the Monterey Boating Club building as it appeared during the Great White Fleet's visit of May 1908. On its way around the world, the Great White Fleet became the first battle fleet to circumnavigate the globe. It was from the Boating Club pier that visitors boarded launches for a once-in-a-lifetime visit to Uncle Sam's mighty white armada. Colton Hall Collection.

Opposite the Boating Club building and facing the Steamship Company wharf is Monterey's Custom House. Dating back to the early 1800s, the Custom House is considered by many to be the most historic building in California. The large walled-in yard of the Custom House proved a popular spot for long-ago fishermen to mend, stretch and dry their nets. In the background (to the left) can be seen the popular "Mission Art and Curio Store" of old Monterey. L. Josselyn photo — P. Hathaway Collection.

34

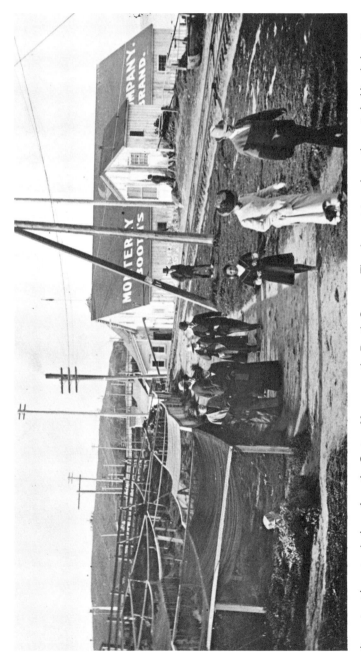

Approximately a stone's throw from the Custom House was the Booth Cannery. The above picture shows the main building before it was destroyed by fire in 1903. Also of interest are several "stylish" Montereyans — perhaps on a Sunday outing — and the net drying racks to the left. Monterey Public Library Collection.

As shown in this 1928 photo (long after the Booth Cannery was rebuilt), the mending of nets often took place in a large field in front of the Booth Cannery complex. L. Josselyn photo — P. Hathaway Collection.

About to unload a catch of sardines, the crew of the lampara boat THAD (with its accompanying lighter — tow boat), are shown alongside the Booth Cannery pier. A portion of the old Monterey wharf is shown in the background. T. Souza Collection.

The Booth Cannery pier presents a different picture when viewed from its seaward end. Taken in 1938, the above photo shows the OLYMPIC (one of Monterey's early purse seiners), as a typical morning fog obscures the background. McKay photo & Collection.

The Booth Cannery complex as it appeared from Fisherman's Wharf. In the foreground is the lampara boat CATERINA, and to the right are three early Monterey fishermen diligently at work in a lighter. P. Hathaway Collection.

37

P. Hathaway Collection.

P. Hathaway Collection.

P. Hathaway Collection.

38

The series of pictures on these two pages illustrate the unloading process of a heavily loaded lighter. Her hold filled with sardines and riding low in the water, the lighter S. OYAMA (as pictured in these four photos) is secured to the Booth Cannery pier. P. Hathaway Collection.

A rare picture of a Pacific Coast Steamship Company vessel alongside its Monterey facility. The photo is thought to have been taken around 1910 and shows a portion of the Booth Cannery pier to the far right. F. Swain photo — Monterey Public Library Collection.

Fisherman's Wharf and a portion of the Booth Cannery (not to mention a parade of vintage automobiles), as they appeared from Presidio curve in August of 1919 (during the Pacific Fleet's visit to Monterey Bay). A. Heidrick photo — Monterey Public Library Collection.

41

As the years rolled on, the transformation of the Steamship Company pier to an all-purpose wharf was slow and gradual — but certainly impressive. The interesting photo above (which appears here as two separate pictures) was taken from the Booth Cannery roof, and shows Fisherman's Wharf and the Monterey harbor long before Municipal Wharf No. 2 was built. A. Heidrick photo — Monterey Public Library Collection.

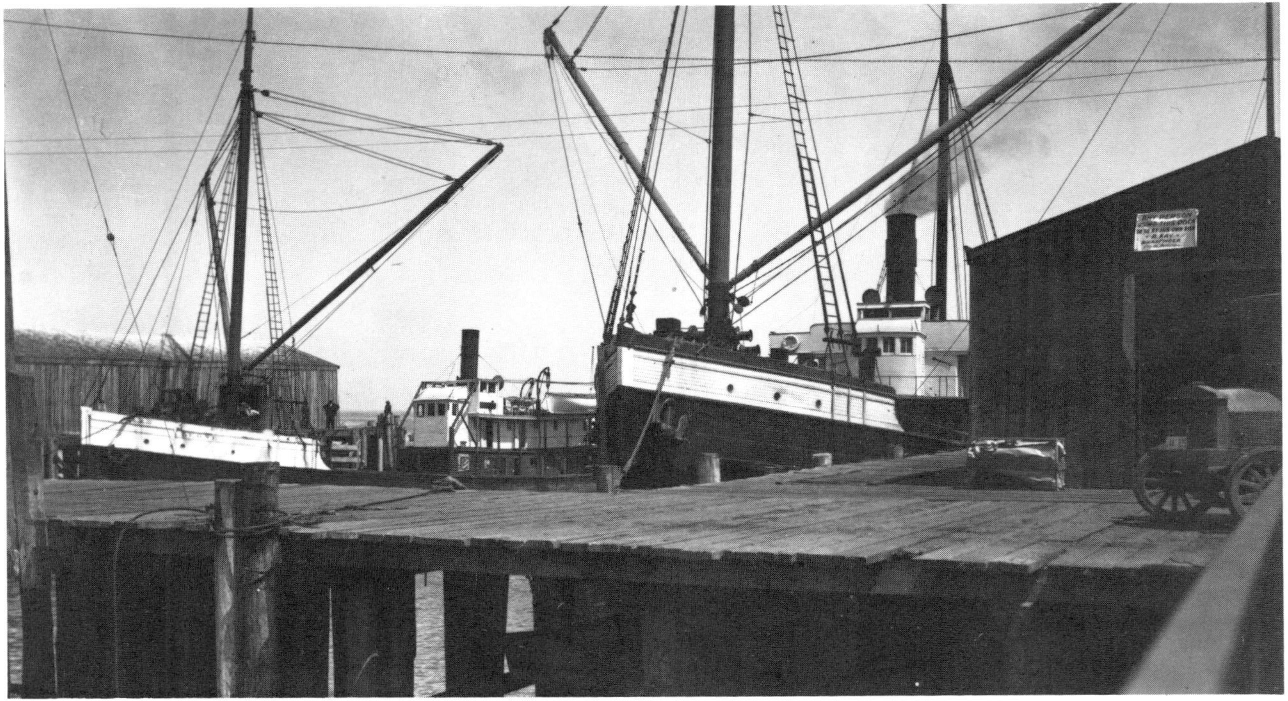

Taken in July of 1926, the above picture shows the coastal freighters CLEONE (left) and DAISY FREEMAN as they were moored at the freighter facilities of Monterey's Wharf No. 1. L. Josselyn photo — P. Hathaway Collection.

The rare photo shown above dates back to the year 1912, and shows portions of two Monterey wharves and/or piers. To the left is an Associated Oil Company tanker moored to the oil company pier (see below and next page for additional oil wharf photos and information). To the right is the reinforced (with railroad track) Monterey and Salinas Valley Railroad Company "Depot Wharf". Originally built in 1874, and measuring 1,300 feet in length, the pier had shrunk considerably in size by 1912. L. Slevin photo — Monterey County Library Collection.

Completed in November of 1904, the Associated Oil Company pier (officially known as the Coalinga Oil and Transportation Company Wharf) was built in the same area as the present day Monterey breakwater. The three-masted vessel pictured to the right of the tugboat (center of picture) is the converted oil barge RODERICK DHU which was lost to the rocks and sand of the Monterey Peninsula's Asilomar Beach in 1909. Behind the RODERICK DHU (and difficult to see) is the four-masted ship MARION CHILCOT. The steamer tied to the far end of the pier is unidentified. Colton Hall Collection.

44

A later view of the Associated Oil Company wharf (note power lines and pole), shows an unidentified coastal freighter to the left, and the masts of a much larger vessel on the pier's opposite side. The oil pier was 650 feet long, it contained 200,000 feet of lumber (exclusive of piles), and it was destroyed by fire during the Monterey oil tank fire of 1924. J. Oliver photo — Monterey Public Library Collection.

The construction of Monterey's much-needed Municipal Wharf No. 2 got its start in the quarter century year of 1925. Monterey Public Library Collection.

By May of 1926 the size and shape of Monterey's 1,750-foot Wharf No. 2 was apparent to all. Monterey Public Library Collection.

Upon its completion, Wharf No. 2 — boasting a 50 x 310-foot fireproof warehouse at its end — became a busy place. The masts of three coastal freighters can be counted in this picture, with assorted lighters, trollers and lampara boats seen in the foreground. Monterey Public Library Collection.

Shown in this early 1927 Wharf No. 2 photo is a "modern" tractor-trailer rig and a load of Hovden's Portola brand sardines. The coastal freighter CRESCENT CITY (to the left) was a regular on the San Francisco to Monterey run. It is of interest to note that on July 7, 1927, the CRESCENT CITY, while on her way to Monterey to take on a load of sardines, became lost in a dense coastal fog and was wrecked on Monterey Bay's north shore (approximately four miles north of the Santa Cruz lighthouse). Monterey Public Library Collection.

47

Allen Knight Maritime Museum Collection.

On March 17, 1928, the largest ship ever to have docked at Wharf No. 2 (up to that time), arrived in the Monterey harbor. With a cargo of 872 tons of tin plate for the American Can Company (located near Cannery Row), the 10,000-ton freighter ROBIN GOODFELLOW dwarfed Monterey's new wharf. Allen Knight Maritime Museum Collection.

48

With her docking and unloading operations witnessed by hundreds of local residents, the ROBIN GOODFELLOW proved — beyond doubt — that Monterey's Municipal Wharf No. 2 was capable of handling huge ocean-going freighters. Monterey Public Library Collection.

A closer look at the unloading operations of the freighter ROBIN GOODFELLOW. Monterey Public Library Collection.

49

Taken in 1928 (as were the preceding pictures of the freighter ROBIN GOODFELLOW), the above illustration shows Wharf No. 2 in the background. To the left is the original Monterey Boating Club building as it appeared as the popular "Pop Ernest" restaurant. The platform in the foreground is part of "Ferrante's Landing", and was used by local fishermen for a variety of purposes (see following caption for additional Ferrante's Landing information). L. Josselyn photo — P. Hathaway Collection.

In looking toward the Custom House from Pop Ernest's restaurant, one sees boat skids, used for hauling up boats prior to their repair, and Ferrante's Landing to the left. Ferrante's Landing was built in 1902 by Peter Ferrante with the cooperation of the Booth Company. The platform was originally built to serve the lampara boats. As time went on, the landing was used to store skiffs (see skiffs on hoists), with the deck area used to mend and dry nets. The landing was torn down in 1938 for firewood. P. Hathaway Collection.

As previously indicated, the original Monterey Boating Club building near the entrance of Fisherman's Wharf eventually became the home of the Pop Ernest restaurant. The above scene was taken from the Custom House gardens and shows the building — complete with a rear addition — as it took on a "touristy" look. Pop Ernest is well remembered in the Monterey area and is known as the man who originated and perfected the abalone steak. The building was destroyed by fire in 1975. D. Mineo Collection.

51

Monterey's Fisherman's Wharf as seen from the west side (opposite the Pop Ernest restaurant building). Taken in the late 1920s, this view also shows a portion of the Booth Cannery to the left. L. Josselyn photo — P. Hathaway Collection.

52

Later in years, from a similar vantage point, the above photo shows considerable changes to Fisherman's Wharf. An aging Booth Cannery is seen to the left. Monterey Public Library Collection.

G. Seideneck photo — P. Hathaway Collection.

Similar scenes, taken at different times from slightly different locations, show the west side of Fisherman's Wharf. The Critchlow boat hoist, machine shop (to its right), and repair area is prominent in both photos. No date is given for the top photo, with 1947 being listed as the year the bottom picture was taken. F. Harbick photo — P. Hathaway Collection.

54

Rounded tanks, rusted stacks, weathered pilings and waiting skiffs add a nostalgic touch to this view of Wharf No. 1. The tank in the foreground (left) was a hot water tank. The hot water was used for a variety of purposes, including the tanning of nets and the cooking of anchovies. (Anchovies are defined as a small fish of the herring family, referred to by some as a small sardine.) G. Seideneck photo — P. Hathaway Collection.

Looking toward shore, this 1947 picture shows Fisherman's Wharf from a seldom photographed angle. The Harbor House complex is seen at the far end. F. Harbick photo — P. Hathaway Collection.

55

This early picture of Fisherman's Wharf east side (looking toward shore) shows the lampara boat PLEASURE in the foreground. P. Hathaway Collection.

Taken at a later date than the above photo, a more complete picture of the east side of Monterey's Wharf No. 1 is shown. L. Josselyn photo — P. Hathaway Collection.

In this still later view of Wharf No. 1's east side, one sees a scene similar to the scenes shown on the opposite page. Except for minor changes, a few signs and a little paint, the scenes remained strikingly similar over the years. G. Seideneck photo — P. Hathaway Collection.

Clustered around a loading ramp and platform on Fisherman's Wharf are skiffs of assorted shapes and sizes from Monterey's famed purse seiner fleet. F. Harbick photo — P. Hathaway Collection.

From crowds of skiffs to crowds of people. Shown above is one of Monterey's great community gatherings. Celebrating the end of a successful season, local boat owners and fishermen put on a never-to-be-forgotten feed for the people of Monterey. 1937 was the year, Wharf No. 2 was the site, and $13,000 was the cost. R. Ruppel photo — Monterey Peninsula Herald Collection.

W. Morgan photo — D. Mineo Collection.

The blessing of the fleet — a part of Monterey's traditional Santa Rosalia Festival — is an important event on the Monterey Peninsula, and originally took place "at the time of the full moon" in the month of September. Shown above are two illustrations of the blessing of the fleet ceremonies. The pictures were taken on different years, by different photographers, with both pictures having been taken on Wharf No. 2 (looking in opposite directions). L. Blaisdell photo — Monterey Public Library Collection.

59

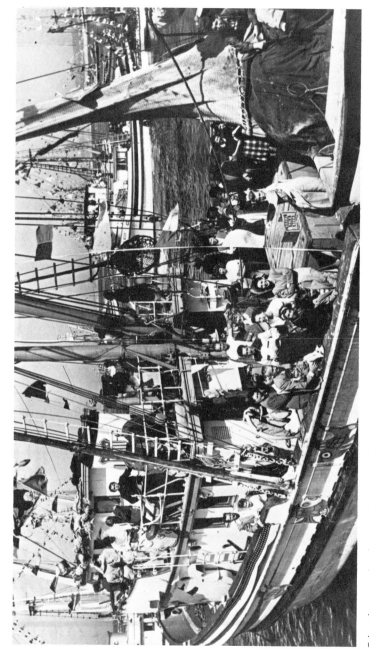

Other than parades, feasts and assorted other events, Monterey's fishing fleet was a colorful part of the Santa Rosalia Festivals. The boat pictured is the purse seiner U.S. LIBERATOR. L. Blaisdell photo — Monterey Public Library Collection.

R. Blaisdell photo & Collection.

As the crowds from the festivals and the blessing of the fleet ceremonies dwindled, the fishermen of old Monterey gathered in quiet corners of Fisherman's Wharf. It was in these quiet corners that they played cards, enjoyed the sunshine and talked about fishing and their experiences at sea. W. Morgan photo — J. Stracuzzi Collection.

As the years rolled on and good friends departed. . . the gatherings grew smaller and the memories perhaps became somewhat faded. W. Morgan photo — J. Stracuzzi Collection.

62

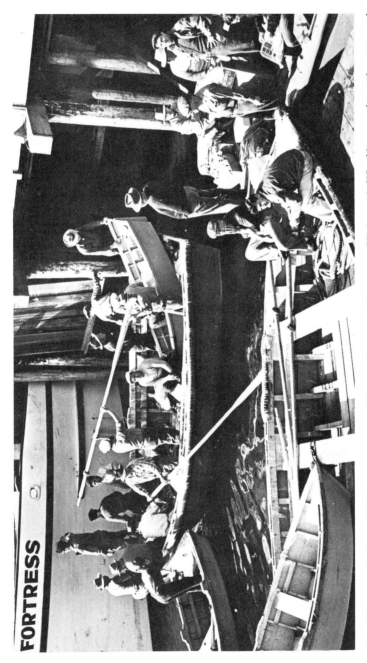

When fish were in the bay and fishing season was in full swing, the once quiet corners of Fisherman's Wharf became alive with activity and echoed to the sounds of men about to go to sea. R. Ruppel photo — D. Mineo Collection.

63

Everything must be ready before a boat sets out, as once the sardines were spotted there was no time to make repairs. The men shown above are inspecting the brail net and hoop used to lift the fish from the hold of the ship and transport them to the hopper. (Hoppers were floating boxes — containers — anchored near the canneries. From the hoppers the fish were pumped to the canneries where they were processed.) G. Seideneck photo — P. Hathaway Collection.

After a busy night of fishing, the "morning after" often finds an exhausted crew repairing their nets and preparing for another trip to sea. Tanning tanks of Wharf No. 1 are shown in the background. F. Harbick photo — P. Hathaway Collection.

The half-ring boat SANTA MARIA at the tanning tanks of Wharf No. 1. P. Hathaway Collection.

65

Without strong nets the sardine industry would not have been the success that it was. To help preserve the nets, they were periodically subjected to a tanning process which strengthened the cotton fibers (of which the early nets were made) and greatly enhanced their life span. The tannic solution within the tanks was obtained from the bark of oak trees. In later years the nets were tarred instead of tanned. The above photo and the picture on the opposite page show purse seiner nets in the process of being dipped into the tanning tanks of Wharf No. 1. R. Ruppel photo — D. Mineo Collection.

66

R. Ruppel photo — D. Mineo Collection.

When nets became damaged and were in need of repair, they were often loaded aboard trucks and taken to nearby fields (yards, streets, etc.) where they were stretched, inspected and mended. The above scene showing a net being loaded aboard a truck was taken at Monterey's Wharf No. 2. F. Harbick photo — P. Hathaway Collection.

68

P. Hathaway Collection.

As indicated in the caption on the opposite page (and in various pictures throughout the book), the mending of nets took place "wherever a spot big enough could be found". In the above two pictures crew members make themselves comfortable in a field and go about the task of repairing their nets. P. Hathaway Collection.

G. Seideneck photo — P. Hathaway Collection.

G. Seideneck photo — P. Hathaway Collection.

70

G. Seideneck photo — P. Hathaway Collection.

As graphically illustrated in the series of pictures on these two pages, there is an art to "stacking" a purse seiner net, and it takes a number of the crew — working together — to do the job right. A study of the pictures shows floats of a variety of shapes, sizes and kinds, and the stern section (turntable) of a purse seiner where the nets are kept. G. Seideneck photo — P. Hathaway Collection.

71

R. Reinstedt photo & Collection.

R. Reinstedt photo & Collection.

With the previous series of pictures (pages 70 & 71) having been taken in the 1940s, one perhaps gets the idea that the color, the traditions, and the significance of Monterey as a fishing port is no more. This, however, is untrue, as scenes similar to those pictured above (and on the preceding page) are still to be found on the Monterey waterfront. The scenes shown on these two pages were taken in 1977 on Monterey's Wharf No. 2. R. Reinstedt photo & Collection.

The above scene takes us from the present, and back to the color of the mid-1930s. A favorite of old-timers, the above picture shows a purse seiner crew as they head for their vessel and a night of fishing. F. Harbick photo — P. Hathaway Collection.

Taken in the late 1930s, the above photo shows additional purse seiner crews as they head for their vessels and what they hope to be a profitable night's catch. F. Harbick photo — P. Hathaway Collection.

Said to have been taken in the early 1940s, the above scene, although somewhat similar to the previous two pictures, shows a motor powered skiff and a harbor full of fishing vessels. G. Seideneck photo — P. Hathaway Collection.

R. Ruppel photo — Allen Knight Maritime Museum Collection.

Upon reaching their vessel it was out to sea and in search of fish. Shown above are the large purse seiners JOHN R. and LINA V. as they enter and exit the Monterey harbor. R. Ruppel photo — P. Hathaway Collection.

When the sardines were spotted it was "all hands on deck". In the above scene the fish have been encircled and are secure in the purse (net). The brailing process has begun (lifting the fish from the sea), with the man in the skiff keeping an eye on the net and helping to keep it from closing. R. Ruppel photo — D. Mineo Collection.

A closer look at the man in the skiff. With the oar in his hands (usually a long pole was used) he was able to keep the skiff from drifting too close to the ship. This kept the net open and enabled the brailing process to continue. P. Hathaway Collection.

On occasion, when one vessel caught more than it could haul (or had already reached its limit), the skipper would call in a second vessel and share the catch. In the above scene crew members of the purse seiner CITY OF MONTEREY (right) keep the net taught as men from the CALIFORNIA ROSE prepare to brail the fish. P. Hathaway Collection.

Above is a graphic illustration of brailing. Old-timers describe a brail of this type as "the horn of plenty". After the fish were lifted from the sea they were dumped into the hold of the ship. P. Hathaway Collection.

When a load of sardines was caught and the nets were back aboard the boats, the purse seiners would head for the canneries where the process of brailing the fish into the hoppers would begin. In the above photo Cannery Row is to the far left, and to the far right the crew of the purse seiner SANTA ROSA are brailing fish from the hold of their vessel into a hopper. R. Ruppel photo — P. Hathaway Collection.

With Cannery Row as a backdrop, the above illustration shows that the activity around the hoppers wasn't confined to purse seiners. Pictured are boats and lighters of the squid fishing variety as they wait their turn at the hoppers. R. Ruppel photo — P. Hathaway Collection.

83

R. Ruppel photo — D. Mineo Collection.

R. Ruppel photo — D. Mineo Collection.

84

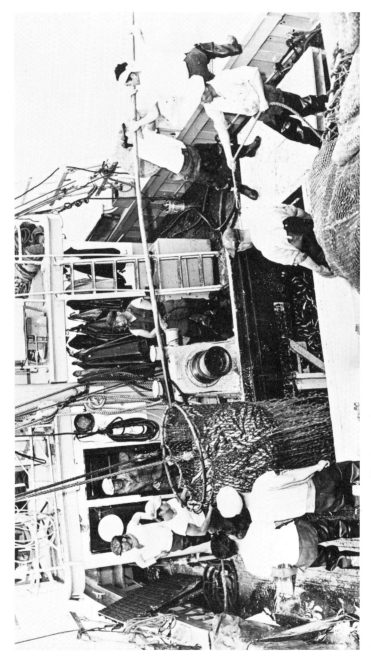

As only pictures can do, the process of brailing fish from a ship's hold is graphically illustrated in the photos on this and the preceding page. R. Ruppel photo — D. Mineo Collection.

Illustrated above and on the opposite page is the brailing of fish from a heavily loaded purse seiner (note the quantity of fish on the deck). It was during these exceptionally good catches that a large purse seiner would often bring in more than 150 tons of sardines. R. Ruppel photo — D. Mineo Collection.

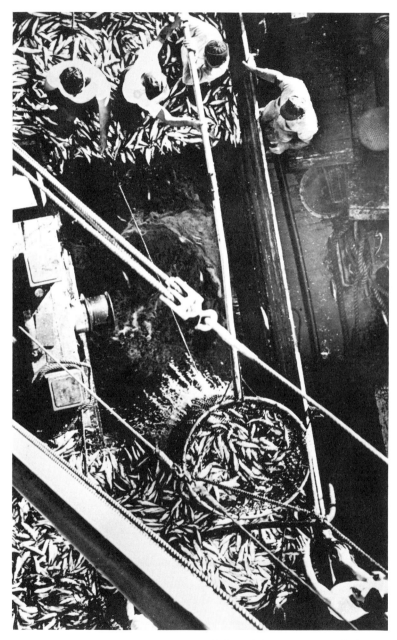

R. Ruppel photo — D. Mineo Collection.

Tied to a buoy off Cannery Row, the purse seiner CALIFORNIA ROSE waits her turn at the hoppers. Filled to capacity with an estimated 160 tons of sardines, this 1936 photo illustrates how low in the water a purse seiner would ride when it was fully loaded with fish. S. Bruno photo — V. Bruno Collection.

Alongside the hopper (as seen in the foreground), the crew of the CALIFORNIA ROSE prepare to brail the fish from the hold of their ship. S. Bruno photo — V. Bruno Collection.

With the crew of the CALIFORNIA ROSE intent on brailing, the above view shows the vessel's deck deep with fish. A member of the crew, who was aboard at the time this 1936 picture was taken, states the CALIFORNIA ROSE was capable of carrying 132 tons of fish in her hold and an additional 28 tons on her decks. S. Bruno photo — V. Bruno Collection.

As previously indicated, and as graphically illustrated in the above aged post card, after brailing the fish from the hold of the ship, they were dumped into hoppers (center) from which they were pumped — via pipes — to the waiting canneries. P. Hathaway Collection.

In the mid-1930s thankful fishermen and delighted Montereyans welcomed the introduction of the short-wave radio to the boats of the local fleet. While the men at sea exchanged pleasantries (or perhaps a few well chosen expletives), the people at home gathered around their marine-band short-wave radios and followed the progress of the fleet. Shown above is a proud Salvatore (Badazza) Russo (a pioneer local user of the short-wave radio), posing with his radio in the pilot house of the purse seiner WESTERN STAR. T. Russo Collection.

While not pertaining to sardines, the above photo shows that not all of the action took place away from the wharves. Shown above is the brailing of squid from the hold of a lampara boat and onto Wharf No. 2. The vessel in the background is the lampara boat SANTA ROSALIA. Monterey Peninsula Herald Collection.

The brailing process continues as the squid are hoisted to a wholesale outlet on Wharf No. 2. Monterey Peninsula Herald Collection.

After a long and tiring fishing trip, the job of climbing into the hold to help with the brailing was not looked forward to by anyone. *Monterey Peninsula Herald* Collection.

As mentioned in the text, the fishing for sardines was most often done at night (when the phosphorescent glow of the fish could best be spotted). Illustrated above and on the following six pages are a series of pictures taken at night, which show the process of "bringing in the fish". After the nets had been set before the oncoming fish, and the sardines "were pursed", the process of drawing in the nets and bringing the fish to the surface began. T. Russo Collection.

As the purse draws tighter, the water becomes alive with fish! T. Russo Collection.

The brailing process begins. T. Russo Collection.

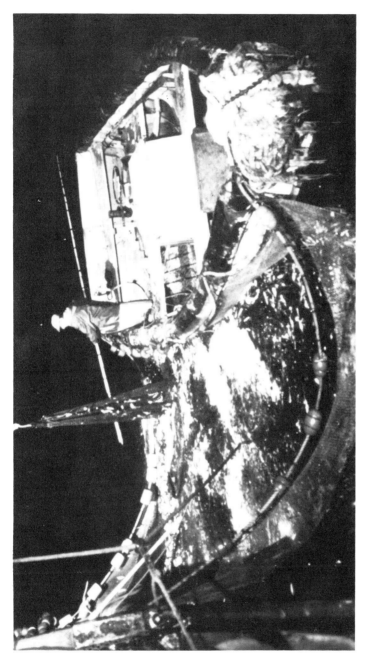

With quick reactions and a sturdy pole, the man in the skiff is able to keep his craft away from the ship, enabling the all-important brailing process to continue. T. Russo Collection.

A few of the sardines were able to flee the confines of the net, but unless the net was damaged or a mistake by the crew was made, the few that got away were not even worth counting. T. Russo Collection.

The brailing process took considerable skill and a lot of hard work. T. Russo Collection.

From the sea to the hold was a one-way trip for the sardine. G. Robinson photo — P. Hathaway Collection.

After the fish were unloaded and the purse seiners were moored, it was back to the wharf for Monterey's men of the sea. G. Seideneck photo — P. Hathaway Collection.

While the fleet rests and waits for another night of fishing, a lone crew member returns to Wharf No. 1 after probable maintenance work aboard his vessel. G. Seideneck photo — P. Hathaway Collection.

From Wharf No. 2, with Fisherman's Wharf and the canneries in the background, Monterey's fishing fleet presents a peaceful picture. L. Blaisdell photo — Colton Hall Collection.

Dated 1928, the above photo shows a variety of boats and an interesting look at Monterey from the sea. Among the vessels pictured are lampara boats, salmon boats, pleasure craft, hook and liners, and lighters. L. Josselyn photo — P. Hathaway Collection.

Closer to shore, and showing a similar view of the Monterey shoreline, the above photo is also thought to have been taken in the late 1920s. The vessel in the foreground has been described as either a Fish and Game boat or a research ship. L. Josselyn photo — P. Hathaway Collection.

Among the mainstays of Monterey's early fishing fleet were boats similar to those pictured above. The four larger vessels are lampara boats, with the skiffs, quite appropriately, being of comparative size. P. Hathaway Collection.

L. Blaisdell photo — Monterey Public Library Collection.

Looking out to sea from Fisherman's Wharf, the harbor scenes changed as did the years. The above two pictures show a peaceful Monterey harbor, boasting several vessels of the purse seiner variety. L. Blaisdell photo — Monterey Public Library Collection.

105

When Monterey was considered "the sardine capital of the world", her harbor was filled with purse seiners of all descriptions. Other than a sky of masts and a crowded harbor, the above photo shows carefully covered nets on the stern sections of the boats. The nets were covered in an effort to help protect and preserve them. G. Seideneck photo — P. Hathaway Collection.

Proud vessels and a picturesque harbor was the story of old Monterey in the late '30s and early '40s. R. Ruppel photo — P. Hathaway Collection.

As time passed, a marine service station was added to the seaward end of Wharf No. 1's tanning tank pier. Shown above is the purse seiner CERRITO BROS. as she prepares to take on fuel. F. Harbick photo — P. Hathaway Collection.

A second view of the marine service station on Wharf No. 1's tanning tank pier also shows the bow of the flag-bedecked purse seiner CAMARELLO. G. Seideneck photo — P. Hathaway Collection.

At the end of Wharf No. 1's second finger pier was also a second marine service station. The above picture was taken in 1947 and shows the small purse seiner THELMA KAY tied to the pier. Allen Knight Maritime Museum Collection.

Also tied to Wharf No. 1's second finger pier is the half-ring boat GERALDINE-ANN.
A happy crew is seen atop the pilot house as an overflow catch of sardines fills the
vessel's deck. Allen Knight Maritime Museum Collection.

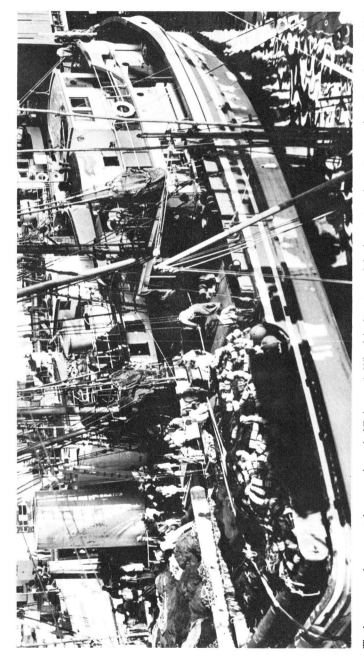

The busy scene above was taken near the end of Fisherman's Wharf, looking toward the finger piers shown in several previous photos. Said to have been taken during a Santa Rosalia Festival, the picture illustrates the size of a large purse seiner, and shows crowds of happy Montereyans as they visit the various vessels. R. Ruppel photo — P. Hathaway Collection.

The purse seiner PETRINA F. moored to Monterey's Wharf No. 1. (The preceding picture was taken from the wharf area near the stern section of this boat.) F. Harbick photo — P. Hathaway Collection.

Taken in September of 1939, the above picture shows the purse seiner BELVEDERE beside Monterey's Wharf No. 2. Allen Knight Maritime Museum Collection.

The above picture was taken in May of 1952 and shows the half-ring boat NYNA ROSE with a larger, and unidentified, purse seiner in the background. Allen Knight Maritime Museum Collection.

114

Originally built for sardines, the ST. MARY, as pictured above, has been converted to a drag boat. N. Vingrad photo — P. Hathaway Collection.

The purse seiner EL PADRE — December 24, 1937. Allen Knight Maritime Museum Collection.

The purse seiner ENDEAVOR as it appeared in 1948. Allen Knight Maritime Museum Collection.

The purse seiner CITY OF MONTEREY — December 24, 1937. Allen Knight Maritime Museum Collection.

The purse seiner STAR OF MONTEREY. Monterey Peninsula Herald Collection.

The Monterey purse seiner came in varying sizes, but, as indicated on the preceding pages, they were of the same basic design. The trim lines of these ships were admired by fishermen from throughout the world, and the owners of the vessels were envied by all.

What would a fishing port be without seagulls? In the above scene the purse seiner SEA GIANT is making its way into the Monterey harbor after unloading fish at the cannery hoppers. As the crew cleaned the boat and threw the sardines overboard that were found on the deck, the ever-present seagulls followed in the vessel's wake and fought over every morsel. Allen Knight Maritime Museum Collection.

One of the best known, and boasting one of the best records, was the purse seiner DIANA. After the sardines were no more, the DIANA, as did the majority of the large purse seiners, headed south and called California's southern waters home. After an absence of many years the DIANA did return to Monterey and, as this book goes to press, she is the only large purse seiner of pre-World War II vintage to call Monterey her home port. Photo inset shows a portion of the DIANA's stern, taken in the Monterey harbor, forty years after the overall view was taken. Allen Knight Maritime Museum Collection — photo inset, R. Reinstedt photo & Collection.

R. Reinstedt photo & Collection.

R. Reinstedt photo & Collection.

R. Reinstedt photo & Collection.

Other than the DIANA, the Monterey harbor of today boasts many vessels with colorful pasts. To capture the romance, the mystique and the personalities of these vessels, and of the fishermen who share their secrets — one must walk among them and listen to their sounds, and to the sounds of the men as they prepare to go to sea. The pictures on these two pages were taken in the Monterey Marina in 1977. R. Reinstedt photo & Collection.

Monterey Public Library Collection.

The scenes of Monterey harbor are not always peaceful. Over the years there have been many storms that have brought havoc to the bay, with the storms of 1915, 1919, 1943 and 1953 being among the best remembered. The above two scenes are of the April 29, 1915 storm in which over 50 vessels were deposited upon the Monterey shores. Monterey Public Library Collection.

According to aged accounts, a total of 93 vessels of assorted shapes and sizes were counted upon the Monterey shores after the November 26, 1919 storm. Monterey Public Library Collection.

Forty boats wound up on the beaches after the December 8, 1943 storm. The above scene was taken from Monterey's Wharf No. 1. Monterey Public Library Collection.

Among the vessels blown ashore during the storm of February 23, 1953, were the two purse seiners NEW HOPE and CERRITO BROS. Shown above, a lone Montereyan braves the breakers as he pulls away from the grounded ships. L. Blaisdell photo — Monterey Public Library Collection.

As the tide receded, the NEW HOPE and the CERRITO BROS. were left high and dry on the Monterey beach (both vessels were eventually salvaged). R. Reinstedt photo & Collection.

Other than storms, fog, treacherous currents, rocky coastlines and unpredictable weather, boat owners and fishermen also had to be concerned about fires. Above is the lampara boat CRIVELLO NO. 1 as she burns in the Monterey harbor. Allen Knight Maritime Museum Collection.

125

With all roads leading to the bay, long before convention complexes and the demise of the sardine changed her ways, Monterey was a busy fishing community with a distinct charm and character all its own. Taken in the late 1920s, the above picture gives a unique view of the old town, with the United States Navy battleship NEW MEXICO in the background. Monterey Public Library Collection.

In rounding Monterey's waterfront and heading toward Cannery Row, one was afforded picturesque vistas of the Monterey wharves and the Booth Cannery complex. The above picture was taken from Presidio hill on July 13, 1928. L. Josselyn photo — P. Hathaway Collection.

Closer to Cannery Row, and taken from Presidio curve, the above view of the Monterey harbor and Wharf No. 2 also offers a snowcapped Mt. Toro as a backdrop. D. Eaton Collection.

Before moving from Monterey harbor to Cannery Row, an aerial view of Wharf No. 1 and the Booth Cannery complex (left of wharf) may help to bring many of the previous pictures into perspective. As it appeared on August 9, 1937, Monterey's Fisherman's Wharf shows little resemblance to the original Pacific Coast Steamship Company pier as it appears on page 26. McKay photo & Collection.

Taken in March of 1938, and at a considerably lower altitude, the above photo again shows Monterey's Wharf No. 1 and the elaborate Booth Cannery complex. McKay photo & Collection.

Closer to Cannery Row (with the San Carlos and E.B. Gross Cannery complexes shown in the lower right corner), the above photo — taken in February of 1938 — shows the Monterey breakwater (completed in 1934), the Booth Cannery, and Monterey's wharves No. 1 and No. 2. Photo inset — taken in March of 1938 — details the beginning of Cannery Row and the San Carlos Cannery (nearest camera) and E.B. Gross Cannery complexes from a second angle. McKay photos & Collection.

C. Tuttle photo — P. Hathaway Collection.

In the same general area of the San Carlos Cannery complex, once stood the "tank farm" of the Associated Oil Company. It was these oil tanks that fed fuel to the tankers that tied up to the oil company wharf (seen to the right of the top photo). On September 14, 1924 lightning hit the storage tanks, resulting in a fire that threatened the entire Monterey waterfront, and did destroy the oil company pier. C. Tuttle photo — P. Hathaway Collection.

131

Soldiers from the Monterey Presidio were used to help fight the 1924 fire, with two losing their lives to the inferno. Aged accounts describe the blaze as "The greatest conflagration in the history of Monterey and one of the greatest oil fires of California." L. Josselyn photo — P. Hathaway Collection.

As seen from Cannery Row, with the Murray mansion in the foreground, billowing clouds of black smoke from Monterey's oil fire darkened the sky . . . , creating considerable concern for the people of the Peninsula, as well as for people in outlying Monterey Bay area communities. P. Hathaway Collection.

Said to have been taken in the early teens, and certainly long before the holocaust of 1924, the above photo shows a portion of Cannery Row in its infancy. Monterey Public Library Collection.

Cannery Row and a portion of the United States Pacific Fleet as seen from the roof of the Publc Library Collection.

UNLOADING FISH
K. HOVDEN CO.
MONTEREY, CAL.

As described by old-timers, the above photo shows the unloading pier of the Hovden Company cannery. The picture was taken when the fish were unloaded by cable, before hoppers came into use. The pier was located at the north end of Cannery Row and was one of the first to be built. T. Souza Collection.

134

Monterey Canning Company warehouse — August 1919. A. Heidrick photo — Monterey

In viewing a second cannery pier, one also sees a variety of early vessels. L. Josselyn photo — P. Hathaway Collection.

A rare view of Cannery Row's canneries and their picturesque piers as seen from the sea. The structures in the foreground are thought to be the Carmel Canning Company complex. With the buildings made of wood and saturated with fish oil, it is not difficult to understand why many were lost to a careless match. . . , or, in later years, perhaps it was an arsonist's torch that ignited the spark. P. Hathaway Collection.

Long after the picture on the opposite page was taken, and as Cannery Row "went modern", fish by the thousands were piped into the canneries from nearby hoppers. Shown above are the fish as they were disgorged from a hopper pipe, to continue their trip, via a fish elevator, to the weighing scale (platform) and cutting tables. G. Robinson photo — P. Hathaway Collection.

When the fish reached the top of the elevator they were dumped on a scale to be weighed. Shown above is an automatic conveyor belt and scale loaded with sardines. G. Robinson photo — P. Hathaway Collection.

In this second view of a fish elevator, one can readily see how the fish were brought into the canneries. . . , while the water was left behind. J. Stracuzzi Collection.

As indicated in the above post card picture (said to have been taken in the mid-teens), during the very early days people of all ages were hired to work in the canneries. As also indicated in the picture, in the early days the heads and tails of the fish were cut off by hand. M. Rieder, Publ., Los Angeles, California.

As time marched on, and as things became automated, the heads and tails of the fish were cut by machines. Shown above are fish being loaded into a cutting machine. G. Robinson photo — P. Hathaway Collection.

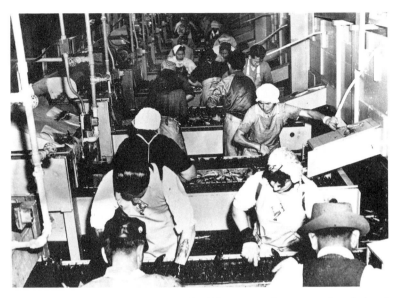

A different view, in a different cannery, of a different type of cutting machine (referred to as a double cutter). R. Ruppel photo — D. Mineo Collection.

At the packing table (also referred to as the canning table), the headless and tailless fish were packed into cans. R. Ruppel photo — D. Mineo Collection.

A second packing table scene shows a group of "Monterey's finest", as they busily fill oval cans with tasty sardines. F. Harbick photo — P. Hathaway Collection.

Unique to this packing table picture is that the fish are being packed into round tall cans (one pound cans), rather than the flat oval containers that had become a trademark of the Monterey sardine. P. Hathaway Collection.

The packing tables came in all shapes and sizes . . . , as did the ladies who worked so diligently at their sides. G. Robinson photo — P. Hathaway Collection.

143

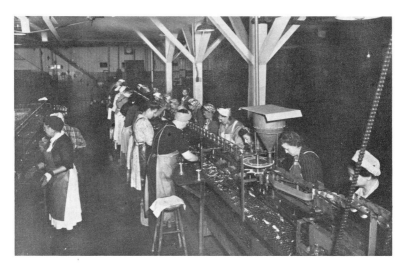

At the packing table (canning line) each can was salted (see funnel-shaped salter in the foreground). From the packing table the cans headed for the steam cookers. F. Harbick photo — P. Hathaway Collection.

From the steam cookers, where the fish received the first of two cooking processes, the cans went through draining machines as pictured above. The machine to the left was for the tall round cans, with the machine in the center being used for the oval cans. The drainers would turn the cans upside down, enabling the excess fish oil, water, etc., to drain out. After the drainers the cans received their final ingredients (such as tomato sauce, mustard, olive oil, etc.) and were sent to the sealing machines. T. Souza Collection.

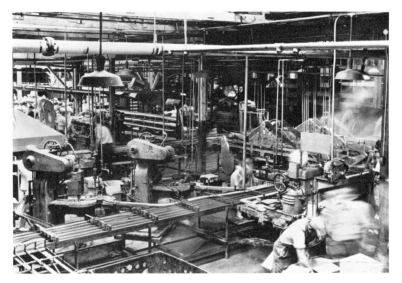

As indicated above, portions of the old canneries were a maze of machinery. The sealing machines (which sealed the lids on the cans) of the Hovden plant are seen in the foreground. Monterey Public Library Collection.

After being sealed the cans were cleaned and placed in large iron containers (baskets). The containers were then wheeled into the cooking chambers (retorts). R. Ruppel photo — P. Hathaway Collection.

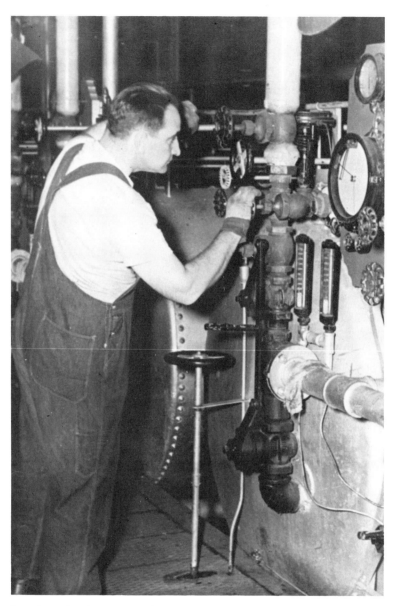

A cooking chamber operator (retort operator) adjusts his gauges as the canned sardines are cooked under pressure. With this being the last phase of the canning process, the fish were then taken to the warehouses where they were labeled and stored. G. Robinson photo — P. Hathaway Collection.

When the Row was "alive" and the fish were being canned in back-to-back shifts, freight trains brought countless box cars to the warehouse sidings. As the railroad cars were filled the sardines were shipped to various locations, soon to be delivered to outlets throughout the nation. T. Souza Collection.

A study of Cannery Row from the air shows the railroad main line and sidings (as described above) as they lead to various warehouses. The picture was taken on August 9, 1937 and shows the northernmost portion of Cannery Row. McKay photo & Collection.

Approximately half of Cannery Row is shown in the above photo, with a portion of New Monterey, Pacific Grove, China Point (Point Cabrillo), Lover's Point and Point Pinos shown in the background. The picture was taken in March of 1938. McKay photo & Collection.

A study of north Cannery Row brings back many memories to old-timers. The elaborate Del Mar Canning Company cannery and warehouse complex is shown in detail as the center point of each photo. McKay photo & Collection.

Cannery Row of the late 1930s was perhaps the busiest, most colorful, noisiest, most profitable, and certainly the smelliest street on the Monterey Peninsula. The overhead walkways that helped to make Cannery Row unique were used primarily to transport the fish from the canneries to the warehouses. G. Seideneck photo — P. Hathaway Collection.

At the north end of Cannery Row was the Hovden Cannery complex. Canning the famed Portola brand sardines, the plant was one of the first to open, and it was the last to close. P. Hathaway Collection.

When no sardines could be found in or around Monterey Bay, the men of Monterey's fishing fleet headed south. It was in these days — with hopes and prayers of better things to come — that the Row was kept alive with sardines that were trucked in from more profitable fishing grounds off the southern California coast. F. Harbick photo — P. Hathaway Collection.

Looking south (from the area of the Hovden Cannery complex) one sees a dying Cannery Row. Wing Chong's grocery store (made famous by the John Steinbeck novel "Cannery Row") can be seen to the right. Also to the right is the Cypress Cafe — proudly advertising "tables for ladies"! F. Harbick photo — P. Hathaway Collection.

The above illustration was taken slightly south of the Hovden complex and directly opposite the Marine Biological Laboratory of Ed "Doc" Ricketts (again of Steinbeck fame). The truck is loaded with such Cannery Row hardware as fish trays and fish cooling containers (baskets). To the right is the original site of Flora's Lone Star "house of pleasure". . . , certainly well known (locally) long before Steinbeck immortalized the establishment in his 1945 novel "Cannery Row". T. Souza Collection.

Sandwiched between two large cannery and warehouse buildings was the Marine Biological Laboratory — and home — of Ed Ricketts. Known to countless Steinbeck fans as "Doc", Ed Ricketts was a unique Cannery Row personality and is fondly remembered by several local residents. Unfortunately, 1948 marked the end of the line for Ricketts as a Southern Pacific train hit his car — killing Doc — at a crossing near his Cannery Row home. Today the original "Doc's Lab" is a private men's club. R. Reinstedt photo & Collection.

153

Members of the men's club of old Doc's Lab, as well as merchants and land owners up and down Cannery Row, fear the fires that repeatedly strike the aged and decaying buildings that still dot the Row. The above scene shows a "street scene" of the 1951 Westgate-Sun Harbor Cannery and warehouse fire. The Westgate-Sun Harbor cannery complex was originally known as the Del Mar Canning Company. W. Morgan photo — P. Hathaway collection.

When viewed from the tracks it takes little imagination to see why the warehouse buildings of the Westgate-Sun Harbor complex were declared a total loss. As mentioned in the text, with the loss of the buildings, $1,500,000 worth of canned fish also went up in flames. The building to the left was originally a fish reduction plant. W. Morgan photo — P. Hathaway Collection.

As the years rolled on, so too did the fires. In 1953 it was the Custom House Packing Company cannery that was added to the list of fire ravaged buildings. R. Ruppel photo — P. Hathaway Collection.

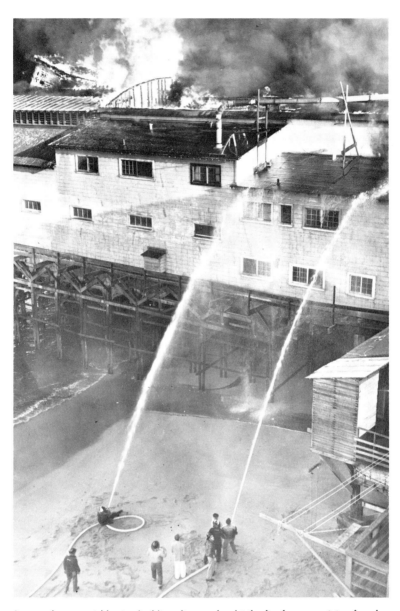

As seen from a neighboring building, firemen fought the fire from a variety of angles. Unfortunately the flames of the Custom House Packing Company proved a stubborn match for the modern fire fighting equipment. W. Morgan photo — P. Hathaway Collection.

As if taking turns, in 1956 the San Carlos Cannery (at the Row's south end) was lost in a dramatic night fire. R. Blaisdell photo & Collection.

Silhouetted against fire, water and smoke, firemen did all in their power to keep the San Carlos Cannery fire from spreading. R. Blaisdell photo & Collection.

The "morning after" leaves nothing to the imagination, as a ghostly fishing fleet is seen through the charred remains of the San Carlos Cannery building. R. Blaisdell photo & Collection.

Shown above is the Row, as seen from the Monterey breakwater. To the extreme left is where the San Carlos Cannery stood. R. Blaisdell photo & Collection.

A closer look at the weathered buildings of the Row's backside, as seen from the San Carlos Cannery shore. R. Blaisdell photo & Collection.

With an abundance of weathered wood, rotting pilings, rusted metal and broken windows. . . , one has to look no further to see that portions of the Row have long since been lost to the elements. R. Reinstedt photo & Collection.

Eyeless windows stare out to sea as old Cannery Row buildings watch and wait for the long-gone sardine. R. Reinstedt photo & Collection.

R. Reinstedt photo & Collection.

Long ago, when the canneries were bustling and bursting with fish, many workers lived in nearby cottages. . . , waiting for the signal that would call them to work. As blasts from the cannery whistles announced that the fish had arrived (or that a new shift was about to begin), the cannery workers would drop what they were doing and head for the hustle and bustle of the Row. R. Reinstedt photo & Collection.

163

The echo of the cannery whistles have long since died and aged Cannery Row signs have long since lost their meaning and their legibility. R. Reinstedt photo & Collection.

As the weeds grew and the metal rusted, the Row sat silent. . . waiting for days that would be no more. R. Blaisdell photo & Collection.

Buildings — with boards and wire covering broken windows — survive for the photographer and for aged Montereyans. . . reminding them of yesterday. . . and perhaps the day before. R. Blaisdell photo & Collection.

Aged and unused loading ramps lead to overgrown sidings as memories linger along the Row. Today, scattered among the derelict buildings, one finds unique shops, gourmet restaurants, seaside vistas and noisy night spots. The streets are again crowded and the people are again there. . . . but Cannery Row of yesterday has long since gone. . . as did the sardine that made it what it was. R. Blaisdell photo & Collection.

Summary

As "Where Have All the Sardines Gone?" comes to a close, the author wishes to emphasize that a work of this type, in a format of this size, can only be considered an introduction to the Monterey waterfront and to the color and drama of Monterey's famed fishing industry. With this work serving as little more than a brief overview of the times, troubles and triumphs of the industry and its people, it is hoped by the author that a larger publication will, at some future date, follow. . . a publication that will do justice to the colorful and complex years of the sardine industry and to the personalities who made it what it was.